dinopix

Teruhisa Tajima

CHRONICLE BOOKS

SAN FRANCISCO

First published in the United States
in 1995 by Chronicle Books.
First published in Japan in 1994
by Kadokawa Shoten Publishing Co., Ltd., Tokyo.

English language rights arranged with Kadokawa
Shoten Publishing Co., Ltd., Tokyo, through Japan
UNI Agency, Inc.

Printed in Hong Kong.
ISBN: 0-8118-1155-7

Library of Congress Cataloging-in-Publication
Data available.

Cover and text design: Geordie Stephens
Book design: Shoko Abe for Thesedays Inc.
Dinosaur images supplied by: Kaiyodo Co., Ltd.
Original dinosaur design: Shinobu Matsumura,
Kazunari Araki, and Teruhisa Tajima

Distributed in Canada by
Raincoast Books
8680 Cambie Street
Vancouver, B.C. V6P 6M9

10 9 8 7 6 5 4 3 2 1

Chronicle Books
275 Fifth Street
San Francisco, California 94103

contents

Ankylosaurus **on the railway**

family: Ankylosauridae • infraorder: Ankylosauria • suborder: Thyreophora • order: Ornithischia •
length: 33 feet • height: 7.5 feet • weight: 4 tons • diet: herbivorous (herbaceous plants) •
age: 35 • habitat: North America, Australia (mountainous regions) • nature: sensitive, but not aggressive •
features: body armor made of bone, and a tail that can be used as a club against enemies

Velociraptor in New Zealand

family: Dromaeosauridae • infraorder: Tetanurae • suborder: Theropoda • order: Saurischia •
length: 5.94 feet • height: 3.3 feet • weight: 110 lbs. • diet: carnivorous •
habitat: Asia, North America, Australia • nature: probably highly dangerous to human beings •
features: probably highly intelligent; sociable; each year several of its victims are found

Tyrannosaurus in San Francisco

family: Tyrannosauridae · infraorder: Tetanurae · suborder: Theropoda · order: Saurischia · length: 46.2 feet ·
height: 18.48 feet · weight: 7 tons · diet: carnivorous · habitat: North America, Australia, Central Asia ·
age: 40+ · nature: ferocious, but never attacks human beings · features: sensitive to noise and environmental pollution

Diplodocus on the atoll of Mana Island

family: Diplodocidae • infraorder: Sauropoda • suborder: Sauropodomorpha • order: Saurischia •
length: 89.1 feet • height: 36.3 feet • weight: 11 tons • diet: herbivorous (tree leaves, ferns) •
habitat: North America • age: 90 • nature: mild, never becomes aggressive •
features: very lightweight dinosaur for its size

Barosaurus in Edmonton

family: Diplodocidae • infraorder: Sauropoda • suborder: Sauropodomorpha • order: Saurischia •
length: 82.5 feet • height: 49.5 feet (they are able to guard their vulnerable young against attack from hungry
allosaurid theropods) • weight: 12 tons • diet: herbivorous (tree leaves, ferns) • habitat: North America, Africa •
age: 110 • nature: mild, but becomes aggressive against enemies

Chasmosaurus by the sea

family: Ceratopsidae • infraorder: Ceratopsia • suborder: Marginocephalia • order: Ornithischia •
length: 16.5 feet • height: 5.94 feet • weight: 2.5 tons • diet: herbivorous (fibrous plants) •
habitat: North America, Australia, Central Asia (highlands) • age: 40 •
nature: rude and terrifying if made angry; it is no easy match even for Tyrannosaurus,
a worthy opponent • features: large bony neck frill

Pteranodon over San Francisco

family: Pteranodonidae • suborder: Pterodactyloidae • order: Pterosauria • span: 22.94 feet •
length: 7.92 feet • weight: 36.52 lbs. • diet: fish • habitat: North America (coastal regions) •
age: 12 • nature: capricious • maximum flightspeed: 30 mph (they can fly over 90 miles) •
features: sociable; it can scarcely flap its wings, only glide

Brachiosaurus

on Bora Bora Island

family: Brachiosauridae • infraorder: Sauropoda •
suborder: Sauropodomorpha • order: Saurischia •
length: 74.25 feet • height: 42.9 feet •
weight: 77 tons • diet: herbivorous (conifers,
cycads, ferns) • habitat: North America, Africa,
Europe • age: 130 • nature: mild and friendly,
but becomes aggressive when attacked •
features: although unable to stand on its hind legs
because of its heavy weight, it can eat leaves at
treetop by using its very long neck

Allosaurus in the desert of Western Australia

family: Allosauridae • infraorder: Tetanurae • suborder: Theropoda • order: Saurischia •
length: 36.3 feet • height: 14.19 feet • weight: 2 tons • diet: carnivorous • habitat: North America,
Africa, Australia • age: 25 • nature: very ferocious, frequently attacks human beings •
speed: approximately 10.8 mph; recently, its numbers have decreased

Triceratops at North Rim, Grand Canyon

family: Ceratopsidae • infraorder: Ceratopsia • suborder: Marginocephalia • order: Ornithischia •
length: 29.7 feet • height: 13.2 feet • weight: 5.4 tons • diet: herbivorous (fibrous plants) •
habitat: North America • age: 50 • nature: rude and terrifying if made angry; it is no easy match
even for Tyrannosaurus, a worthy opponent

Ankylosaurus on a canyon road

family: Ankylosauridae • suborder: Ankylosauria • order: Ornithischia • length: 33 feet •
height: 7.59 feet • weight: 4 tons • diet: herbivorous (herbaceous plants) •
habitat: North America, Australia (mountainous regions) • age: 40 • nature: sensitive, but not aggressive •
features: body armor made of bone, and a tail that can be used as a club against enemies

Iguanodon on the beaches of Oahu

family: Iguanodontidae • suborder: Ornithopoda • order: Ornithischia • length: 33 feet •
height: 18.15 feet • weight: 4.5 tons • diet: herbivorous (horsetails, ferns, possibly flowering plants) •
habitat: Europe, North America • age: 40 • nature: comparatively mild, but becomes aggressive
when attacked • features: socializes in large groups, and lives a nomadic life

Allosaurus in southeastern Utah

family: Allosauridae • infraorder: Tetanurae • suborder: Theropoda • order: Saurischia • length: 36.3 feet • height: 14.19 feet • weight: 1.5 tons • diet: carnivorous • habitat: North America, Africa, Australia • age: 27 • nature: very ferocious, frequently attacks human beings • speed: approximately 10.8 mph; recently its numbers have decreased

Stegosaurus on an ice field

family: Stegosauridae • infraorder: Stegosauria • suborder: Thyreophora •
order: Ornithischia • length: 29.7 feet • height: 9.9 feet • weight: 2 tons •
diet: herbivorous (low-growing plants) • habitat: North America (mountainous regions) •
age: 60 • features: two rows of bony plates from neck to tail

Arsinoitherium, 5:59 P.M.

family: Arsinoitheridae • order: Embrithopoda • subclass: Theria • length: 10.5 feet •
height: 5.94 feet • weight: 1.5 tons • diet: herbivorous (tree leaves) • habitat: Africa, North America •
age: 18 • nature: rude and aggressive • features: not very smart

Tyrannosaurus in the darkness (with Pteranodon)

family: Tyrannosauridae • infraorder: Tetanurae • suborder: Theropoda • order: Saurischia • length: 46.2 feet •
height: 18.48 feet • weight: 7 tons • diet: carnivorous • habitat: North America, Australia, Central Asia •
age: 40+ • nature: ferocious, but never attacks human beings •
features: sensitive to noise and environmental pollution

Diplodocus on the shore

family: Diplodocidae • infraorder: Sauropoda • suborder: Sauropodomorpha • order: Saurischia •
length: 82.5 feet • height: 39.6 feet • weight: 11 tons • diet: herbivorous (tree leaves, ferns) •
habitat: North America • age: 110 • nature: mild, never becomes aggressive •
features: very lightweight dinosaur for its size

Stegosaurus at Dead Horse Point, Arizona

family: Stegosauridae • infraorder: Stegosauria • suborder: Thyreophora • order: Ornithischia •
length: 29.7 feet • height: 9.98 feet • weight: 2 tons • diet: herbivorous (low-growing plants) •
habitat: North America (mountainous regions) • age: 60 •
features: two rows of bony plates from neck to tail

Brachiosaurus

at Monterey Beach

family: Brachiosauridae • infraorder: Sauropoda •
suborder: Sauropodomorpha • order: Saurischia •
length: 69.3 feet • height: 39.6 feet • weight: 70 tons •
diet: herbivorous (conifers, cycads, ferns) •
habitat: North America, Africa, Europe •
age: 100 • nature: mild and friendly, but becomes
aggressive when attacked •
features: although unable to stand on its hind legs
because of its heavy weight, it can eat leaves at
treetop by using its very long neck

Tyrannosaurus in Hollywood I

family: Tyrannosauridae • infraorder: Tetanurae • suborder: Theropoda • order: Saurischia • length: 42.9 feet • height: 17.82 feet • weight: 6 tons • diet: carnivorous • habitat: North America, Australia, Central Asia • age: 25+ • nature: ferocious, but never attacks human beings • features: sensitive to noise and environmental pollution

Rhamphorhynchus in West Los Angeles

family: Rhamphorhynchusidae • suborder: Rhamphorhynchoidae • order: Pserosauria • span: 5.78 feet • length: 34.4 inches • diet: fish (especially herring) • habitat: Africa, Europe • age: 8 • nature: cowardly, sensitive • maximum flight range: unknown, but probably very large • features: lives in groups by the sea or a lake

Brachiosaurus on Manhattan Beach

family: Brachiosauridae • infraorder: Sauropoda • suborder: Sauropodomorpha • order: Saurischia • length: 66 feet • height: 36.3 feet • weight: 50 tons • diet: herbivorous (conifers, cycads, ferns) • habitat: North America, Africa, Europe • age: 130 • nature: mild and friendly, but becomes aggressive when attacked • features: although unable to stand on its hind legs because of its heavy weight, it can eat leaves at treetop by using its very long neck

Plesiosaurus on Viti Levu, Fiji

superfamily: Plesiosauridae • order: Plesiosauria • length: 13.2 feet •
width: 6.93 feet • weight: 242 lbs. • diet: fish • habitat: Europe, Pacific Ocean •
age: 20 • nature: sensitive, but aggressive against enemies •
features: cannot swim quickly, but can move with agility

Tyrannosaurus in Port Douglas

family: Tyrannosauridae • infraorder: Tetanurae • suborder: Theropoda • order: Saurischia • length: 42.9 feet • height: 18.48 feet • weight: 6 tons • diet: carnivorous • habitat: North America, Australia, Central Asia • age: 30 • nature: ferocious, but never attacks human beings • features: sensitive to noise and environmental pollution

Allosaurus by Lake Powell (with Tyrannosaurus)

family: Allosauridae • infraorder: Tetanurae • suborder: Theropoda • order: Saurischia •
length: 39.6 feet • height: 14.19 feet • weight: 2 tons • diet: carnivorous •
habitat: North America, Africa, Australia • age: 30+ •
nature: very ferocious, frequently attacks human beings •
speed: approximately 10.8 mph; recently its numbers have decreased

Quetzalcoatlus in the sky

family: Azhdarchidae • suborder: Pterodactyloidea • order: Pterosauria • span: 39.6 feet •
length: 28.05 feet • weight: 189.2 lbs. • diet: dead animals, carcasses • habitat: North America, Europe •
age: 20 • nature: cunning • maximum flight speed: 33 mph • flight range: over 90 miles •
features: sociable; can scarcely flap its wings

Camarasaurus **by Lake Ontario**

family: Camarasauridae • infraorder: Sauropoda • suborder: Sauropodomorpha • order: Saurischia •
length: 59.4 feet • height: 19.8 feet • weight: 20 tons • diet: herbivorous (tree leaves, ferns) •
habitat: North America, Europe • age: 90 • nature: usually mild, but frequently becomes aggressive •
features: cannot move very quickly

Brachiosaurus
on Route 15

family: Brachiosauridae • infraorder: Sauropoda •
suborder: Sauropodomorpha • order: Saurischia •
length: 75.9 feet • height: 44.55 feet •
weight: 80 tons • diet: herbivorous (conifers, cycads,
ferns) • habitat: North America, Africa, Europe •
age: 5, 80, 110 • nature: mild and friendly, but
becomes aggressive when attacked •
features: although unable to stand on its hind
legs because of its weight, it can eat leaves
at treetop by using its very long neck

Tyrannosaurus in Hollywood II

family: Tyrannosauridae • infraorder: Tetanurae • suborder: Theropoda • order: Saurischia • length: 42.9 feet • height: 17.82 feet • weight: 6 tons • diet: carnivorous • habitat: North America, Australia, Central Asia • age: 25 • nature: ferocious, but never attacks human beings • features: sensitive to noise and environmental pollution

Unidentified Dinosaur

family: unknown • infraorder: unknown • suborder: unknown • order: unknown • length: 75.9 feet • height: 33 feet • weight: 9.8 tons • diet: herbivorous (tree leaves, ferns) • habitat: North America • age: 80 • nature: mild, never becomes aggressive • features: very lightweight dinosaur for its size

Saltasaurus at Badlands National Park

family: Titanosauridae • infraorder: Sauropoda • suborder: Sauropodomorpha • order: Saurischia •
length: 39.6 feet • height: 16.5 feet • weight: 15 tons • diet: herbivorous (plants) • habitat: South America •
age: 80 • nature: mild and calm • features: its back and abdomen are covered by an armor made of bone

Styracosaurus on Cape Cod

family: Ceratopsidae • infraorder: Ceratopsia • suborder: Marginocephalia • order: Ornithischia •
length: 16.5 feet • height: 5.94 feet • weight: 2.5 tons • diet: herbivorous (fibrous plants) • habitat: North America •
age: 40 • nature: rude and terrifying if made angry; it is no easy match, even for Tyrannosaurus, a worthy opponent •
features: large bony frill spikes

Brachiosaurus on the island of Hawaii

family: Brachiosauridae • infraorder: Sauropoda • suborder: Sauropodomorpha • order: Saurischia • length: 72.6 feet • height: 39.6 feet • weight: 65 tons • diet: herbivorous (conifers, cycads, ferns) • habitat: North America, Africa, Europe • age: 90 • nature: mild and friendly, but becomes aggressive when attacked • features: although unable to stand up because of its heavy weight, it can eat leaves at treetop by using its very long neck

Ceratosaurus in an abandoned oil field

family: Ceratosauridae • infraorder: Ceratosauria • suborder: Theropoda •
order: Saurischia • length: 19.8 feet • height: 6.6 feet • weight: 2,090 lbs. •
diet: carnivorous • habitat: North America, Africa • age: 25 • nature: ferocious, smart, and agile •
features: a solitary animal, it is active during the day; rarely attacks human beings

Elasmosaurus in the sea

superfamily: Plesiosauridae • order: Plesiosauria • length: 46.2 feet • width: 17.82 feet •
weight: 1.5 tons • diet: fish • habitat: Asia (Japan), North America • age: 25 •
nature: sensitive, but aggressive against enemies • features: very long neck (about 26.4 feet);
cannot swim very quickly (approximately 6 mph)

Pentaceratops crossing the road

family: Ceratopsidae • infraorder: Ceratopsia • suborder: Marginocephalia • order: Ornithischia •
length: 16.5 feet • height: 6.6 feet • weight: 1.8 tons • diet: herbivorous (fibrous plants) •
habitat: North America, Australia, and Central Asia (highlands) • nature: rude and aggressive

Plesiosaurus rides the big wave

superfamily: Plesiosauridae • order: Plesiosauria • length: 15.18 feet • width: 7.92 feet •
weight: 792 lbs. • diet: fish • habitat: Europe, Pacific Ocean • age: 40 •
nature: sensitive, but aggressive against enemies •
features: cannot swim very quickly, but can move with agility

Chasmosaurus in the evening

family: Ceratopsidae • infraorder: Ceratopsia • suborder: Marginocephalia • order: Ornithischia • length: 17.16 feet • height: 6.93 feet • weight: 2 tons • diet: herbivorous (fibrous plants) • habitat: North America, Australia, and Central Asia (highlands) • nature: rude and aggressive • features: sociable; fights aggressively against enemies; its horn is in great demand and very expensive; today the capture of this animal is firmly prohibited by WWWF

Brachiosaurus in Houston

family: Brachiosauridae • infraorder: Sauropoda • suborder: Sauropodomorpha • order: Saurischia •
length: 74.25 feet • height: 42.9 feet • weight: 80 tons • diet: herbivorous (conifers, cycads, ferns) •
habitat: North America, Africa, Europe • age: 180 • nature: mild and friendly, but becomes aggressive
when attacked • features: although unable to stand on its hind legs because of its heavy weight, it
can eat leaves at treetop by using its very long neck

Plesiosaurus in the waters of Tahiti

superfamily: Plesiosauridae · order: Plesiosauria · length: 13.2 feet · width: 6.6 feet ·
weight: 440 lbs. · diet: fish · age: 30 · habitat: Europe, Pacific Ocean ·
nature: sensitive, but aggressive against enemies ·
features: cannot swim very quickly, but can move with agility

Postscript

In the fall of 1992, I visited the small town of Moab, Utah. I could not put my finger on what was about to propel me forward. I have always been concerned about some undefined feeling within myself. Maybe I was having a life crisis. I became impatient, hoping to find some clarification. Early one morning I visited Arches National Park in Utah. Far off in the orange-colored morning mist, on the other side of the plain, I saw figures of nocturnal raptors hurrying home, exhaling their white breaths. I thought I had seen a *Brachiosaurus* cast the shadow of its long neck, so characteristic of the lightning dragon, on the gigantic rock surface, deeply reddening in the morning sun. When I saw with my own eyes the answers I was about to obtain, I struggled not to be hasty. I felt there would be an abundance of opportunities in the future for taking pictures in that place.

While I was looking up into the skeletons of ancient giants at the Tyrell Museum of Paleontology at Badlands, Alberta, which I happened to visit some five years ago, I unconsciously chanced upon a scenario for bringing them back to life. To be honest with you, I myself was looking forward to this book more than anyone else. Long ago I wanted to really see these mysterious monsters with my own eyes, just as any child wishes to do. I wondered if they might still be around somewhere, if it would be possible to see one during my lifetime, and what on earth they really looked like. I decided I would take photographs if by some stroke of luck I could meet up with them. But I knew what to expect: the quantity of information in our modern age soberly demonstrated that there was little possibility of the existence today of such creatures. As the last possibility of dinosaur life drew closer to zero with no sightings of the creature called "Nessie" along that narrow loch in Scotland, I thought it would not be a bad idea to soon change the scenery I was familiar with in my daily life.

I was particularly eager to reproduce the gigantic creatures whose images had been imprinted on my mind while I was in Moab. I was persistently concerned about how to realize the visions I had of them there. I knew that one way to revive them existed in the cathode-ray tube in front of me. It seemed too simple, but if the desired fantasy can be easily provided through the digital circuitry that is so popular today, then why not take that route? But to reproduce these huge creatures, something like the energy of life was most urgently needed. I resolved to use digital technology to try to reproduce creatures that would appear to be alive, even if enlarged a hundredfold, through the application of natural light to dinosaur replicas, which had been created in the analog world, and adding moistness to their skin, tension and slackness to their muscles, and providing them with eyesight and the ability to bite. It was not a totally convincing solution, but I felt I was onto something. No matter what, the gigantic creatures that suddenly emerged for the first time at Prince Edward Island provided me with possibilities and encouragement.

—Teruhisa Tajima
May, 1994

About the Author

Teruhisa Tajima was born in Japan in 1949. A graduate of the graphic design department of Tama Art University, he worked at the CBS Sony design office for six years, and has been a freelance designer since 1980. In 1988 he began experimenting with digital design and photography. He is the author of several books, all published in Japan.